THE COLORS OF ME
Kambiri's Summer Plan

THE COLORS OF ME

Kambiri's Summer Plan

By Dr. Stephanie Oguchi

Illustrations by Robert Paul Jr.

©2019 by Dr. Stephanie Oguchi

All rights reserved soley by the author. The author guarantees all contents are original and do not infringe upon the legal rights of any other person or work. No part of this book may be reproduced in any form without the permission of the author. The views expressed in this book are not necessarily those of the publisher.

Printed in the United States of America

ISBN-978-1-7330624-0-4

Kambiri (Cam-beer-ree): West African name that means "allow me to join his family"

Wheelchair: A chair with wheels that transport a person who is unable to use their legs to walk or run

Kambiri loved summer time.

It was a few days before the end of school,

and he thought about all the fun he would have.

On the last day of school, Kambiri listened to some kids talk about their summer plans.

"I'm going on a hiking trip," a boy said.

"I'm going to basketball camp," said another boy.

The boys turned to Kambiri and asked, "What will you be doing for the summer, Kambiri?"

He said sadly, "I can't do any of those things, so I'm not sure what I will be doing."

Kambiri was sad because hiking and playing basketball are hard for him to do. Kambiri sits in a wheelchair because he has trouble moving his legs on his own. He moves around using his arms to help push the wheels of his wheelchair.

Kambiri's dad picked him up from school that day and noticed that he was very unhappy. "What's wrong? It is the last day of school and you should be excited," his dad said.

"Everyone is going to have fun this summer except for me. I can't hike or play basketball because I sit in a wheelchair," Kambiri said.

"Just because you sit in a wheelchair, doesn't mean you can't do what the other kids are doing. You have to do things in your own special way. Tomorrow, we are going to meet some old friends of mine for some fun, okay?" "Okay dad," Kambiri replied.

The next morning, Kambiri and his dad arrived at a large gym. Kambiri was surprised to see many kids in wheelchairs just like him. They were bouncing basketballs, hitting volleyballs, swinging tennis rackets, and even climbing a special rock hill.

A man greeted Kambiri's dad and said
"Hi, I'm Coach Ken. Welcome to our gym!"

As Kambiri started to reply, a basketball rolled near his wheelchair.

Kambiri picked up the ball and threw it back to the other boys.

"Wow, nice throw!" one of the boys said.

"Do you want to play with us?"

Kambiri looked at his dad and smiled.

His dad waved for him to go and play with the boys.

Kambiri learned how to do many different activities while sitting in his wheelchair, that summer. If he ever had a bit of trouble, he didn't give up trying and did the best that he could. Kambiri couldn't wait to share the special way he learned to play at the gym with all of his friends at school.

KAMBIRI'S MESSAGE

Hi everyone! I hope you enjoyed my story about the different ways I learned to do activities in my wheelchair. We all do things in our own unique way, and it is important to be confident and accept how others learn too.

Be sure to read the other stories that my friends share about their differences!

PARENT'S CORNER

Let's Learn Together:

Parents, help your child understand that they will learn many great and exciting things everyday. Reassure them that it is okay to talk about having feelings of anxiety, while exploring different ways to try new things. Share experiences with your child about having courage and pride after trying something that is unfamiliar to them.

Activity 1: Define what courage means.

Activity 2: Choose 3 people in the past or present that have shown their courage in different ways. Discuss how each person's courage has helped others and brought positivity to the world.

www.ingramcontent.com/pod-product-compliance
Lightning Source LLC
Chambersburg PA
CBHW041153070526
44584CB00004B/298